Action Sports Library

SKIING ON THE EDGE

Bob Italia

Published by Abdo & Daughters, 6535 Cecilia Circle, Edina, Minnesota 55439.

Library bound edition distributed by Rockbottom Books, Pentagon Tower, P.O. Box 36036, Minneapolis, Minnesota 55435.

Printed in the United States.

Library of Congress Card Cataloging-in-Publication Data

Italia, Robert, 1955-
    Skiing on the edge / written by Bob Italia.
        p.   cm. -- (Action sports)
    Includes bibliographical references (p.   ) and index.
    ISBN 1-56239-231-X
    1. Freestyle skiing -- Juvenile literature.   I. Title.   II. Series: Action sports (Edina, Minn.)
GV854.32.I83   1993
796.93 '7 -- dc20   93-19134
                                                   CIP
                                                   AC

Cover Photo: Allsport.
Inside Photos: Allsport 4, 7, 8, 10, 13, 15, 17, 19, 21, 22, 24, 25, 26.
                Stock Market 27.
                Snow*Runner*® (USA) Inc. 29, 31.

Warning: The series *Action Sports Library* is intended as entertainment for children. These sporting activities should never be attempted without the proper conditioning, training, instruction, supervision, and equipment.

Edited by Rosemary Wallner

CONTENTS

*Freestyle skiing is one of the
most exciting forms of snow skiing.*

SKIING ON THE EDGE

Combining Gymnastics with Ballet

Freestyle skiing is one of the most exciting forms of snow skiing. It combines the athleticism of gymnastics with the grace and beauty of ballet.

But not everyone can ski. At the very least, a freestyle skier needs intermediate skiing skills. Beginners should not attempt freestyle skiing. It takes much practice, training, and instruction to perform the various maneuvers and stunts required in freestyle events.

Before attempting any freestyle skiing, skiers seek expert instruction. The United States Ski Association (USSA) has amateur freestyle competitions and establishes safety standards. The USSA directs skiers to the best freestyle training in their area.

The First Jumps

Norway's former Olympic gold medalist, Stein Eriksen, was one of the first skiers to explore skiing. Eriksen experimented with jumps and flips in the early 1950s. His results led to aerial shows in Sun Valley, Idaho.

Doug Pfeiffer took Eriksen's lead. He taught trick skiing between 1956 and 1962 in "The School of Exotic Skiing." Slowly, more and more skiers pushed themselves—and each other—to learn harder tricks.

In 1971, freestyle skiing became a recognized sport. The Waterville Valley Ski Area in New Hampshire held the National Championships of Exhibition Skiing. There, amateurs and professionals competed against each other in three formalized events: mogul, ballet, and aerial skiing. All three events were combined in a single downhill run.

That same year, the Rocky Mountain Professional Freestyle Championships were held. But instead of the single-run format, all three events were run separately. This set the standard for all future freestyle competitions. After the championships, the term "freestyle skiing" was officially adopted.

Mogul

Ballet

Freestyle skiing is composed of three events.

Aerial

Ski professionals and experts judged performances in all three events. They awarded points in each competition. The skier with the most points at the end of all three competitions was crowned freestyle champion.

The mogul event was judged on style, speed, jumps, and degree of difficulty. In the ballet event, the skier was judged on the degree of difficulty, gracefulness, and choreography. In the aerial event, the skier was judged on the degree of difficulty of the jump, the height and distance of the jump, and the form in the air and landing.

Freestyle competitions popped up all over the country. In 1976, a professional World Cup Tour began. Freestyle competitions had spread throughout the world.

The World Cup Tour began in 1976.

In 1981, the U.S. Freestyle Ski Team was formed. This was the sport's first major step toward becoming an Olympic event. In 1988, freestyle skiing debuted at the Calgary Winter Olympics as a demonstration sport. The best freestyle skiers in the world competed against each other, but the winners did not receive any medals.

By 1991, freestyle skiing had joined the Olympic competitions. Today, the World Cup Tour remains strong, and the sport continues to draw more and more enthusiasts.

The Moguls

Moguls (MOE-gulls) are a series of large bumps on a ski slope. Skiing the moguls is the most physically demanding of the three freestyle events. The path through them is nearly impossible to determine. Once skiers find themselves in the moguls, they must perform a series of quick turns at an ever increasing speed.

Skiing on moguls requires a special technique. Skiers keep their head centered between their shoulders while looking down the slope. Their arms are bent slightly at the elbows and raised out and up. Their hips face forward squarely, and their feet are closer than shoulder width apart.

Moguls are physically demanding.

Before attempting the mogul course, skiers plan their turns in advance by looking at the course. This is called choosing a line. Skiers visualize what they are going to do.

To start the first turn, skiers cut across the top of a mogul in a basic stance. Once they reach the top, they drop their hips, bend their knees, and set the downhill ski edge by turning their knees up into the hill. When the edge catches the hill and stops for an instant, the skiers plant the downhill pole.

The ski tails (ends of the skis) swing in the opposite direction as skiers rebound from the mogul. Skiers steer the ski tips into the trough between the moguls—and get ready for the next turn. They set the edge of the downhill ski on the side of the mogul and repeat the process.

Skiers try to ski one mogul at a time. Once they feel comfortable with this technique, they practice linking each turn.

When skiing moguls, body movements occur from the waist down. The torso remains, for the most part, facing downhill. The knees and ankles do most of the work. Knee and ankle action drive the turns. On the moguls, freestyle skiers don't use their hips or shoulders.

Jumping the Moguls

Once skiers master mogul skiing, they try mogul jumping. Jumping is a natural part of mogul skiing because each mogul is a potential ramp. While mogul jumping is the most fun part of mogul skiing, it is also the most difficult.

Skiers start by choosing a mogul that has a good shelf and a good landing spot. A good shelf is a mogul with a flat top—one that slopes out instead of up. Flat-top moguls make good landing spots as well. Skiers can immediately put their skis on edge and start their next turn without breaking rhythm.

Skiers begin a jump by approaching the mogul. When they reach the shelf, they flatten both skis and make sure their hands are in front of them and their knees are bent. When they reach the lip of the mogul, they extend their body. Once airborne, skiers keep their body in a crouched position.

After they have become comfortable with jumping, skiers add more launching power by straightening their knees and quickly lifting their arms in front of them. (Skiers perform different types of jumps while airborne. See the section on jumping for more information.)

Jumping the moguls.

After performing a jump, skiers prepare to land. Landing in a mogul course is not easy. But if the skiers have previously selected a flat spot, landing will be easier. Skiers absorb the landing impact by relaxing their legs. Their knees bend as they touch down. Once their knees bend, the skiers straighten them as if pushing away from the mogul. This keeps the skiers' upper body from collapsing—and keeps the skiers upright. Skiers put their skis on edge immediately after landing to prepare them for the next mogul.

Freestyle Ballet

Freestyle ballet sounds easy at first. Nothing too difficult here, right? Just a few simple twirls and turns.

But freestyle ballet is much more than that. It requires tremendous balance, coordination, flexibility, timing, and concentration. Some of the tricks are just as spectacular as mogul jumping—and just as difficult. Here are some of the most popular freestyle ballet moves.

The Illusion

The illusion is a basic trick that allows skiers to gracefully turn around 360 degrees. It starts from a basic crossover position (skiing across the hill). Skiers perform the illusion on gentle slopes.

To start the illusion, skiers ski down and across a slope. They pick up the downhill ski and cross it over the front of the uphill ski. Then they transfer their weight to the downhill ski. To start the spin, skiers shift their weight to the ball of their foot and pivot the downhill ski while lifting the uphill ski.

Performing the illusion.

As the skiers continue to pivot, the skis uncross, and the uphill ski points straight up. Skiers turn the uphill ski and plant it on the slope in the opposite direction of the downhill ski. They place their weight on the uphill ski and swing the downhill ski around so it is parallel to the uphill ski. They are now ready to try it again!

Tip-Tails

The tip-tail spin is one of the most dramatic ballet tricks. It allows skiers to spin repeatedly on the tips and tails of their skis as if they are about to lift off from the ground.

Skiers start by pointing one ski up the hill. They point the other down the hill. With their knees bent, they push off the back leg, placing all their weight on the outside edge of the front ski. They swing the back ski around in front of them and keep that ski in the air.

At the same time, the skiers press the tip of the front ski into the slope and push up. They place the tail of the back ski into the slope and continue spinning, holding their arms out for better balance. The skiers twirl on the tip of the front ski and the tail of the back ski. To stop spinning, the skiers release the pressure from the front ski and let the tail return to the slope.

Tip tails.

The Two-Footed Tip Vault
The two-footed tip vault allows skiers to spin around 360 degrees while in the air. Skiers start by skiing across the slope. They quickly set both edges of the skis by turning their knees into the hill.

At the same time, they plant their poles uphill of the skis and raise themselves on the ski tips. They straighten their body as they rise and turn into the air. When they have nearly completed their aerial turn, the skiers remove the poles from the slope and land with their skis together.

Split Pole Flip

The split pole flip allows skiers to perform a complete somersault on their skis. To start, skiers find a gentle slope and ski downhill. They grasp their poles so that the palms of their hands rest over the top of the pole grips.

The skiers plant the poles so that they are slightly wider than shoulder width. To start the flip, skiers lift their right foot in front of them. As they set their right foot back down, they drop their upper body between the poles, leading with their head. Maintaining their grip on the poles, they lift their left leg straight back and begin their flip. They let the left leg lead first. The right leg follows.

When the skiers are completely upside down, they bring both skis together. As they continue to flip, they extend their legs forward. When the skiers have nearly completed the flip, they tuck their chin into their chest and bend their knees to absorb the shock. The momentum of the flip pulls the poles from the slope.

Split pole flip.

The Rock and Roll

The rock and roll is the most dramatic flip. It combines elements of gymnastics, and allows skiers to achieve a greater height when flipping.

To do the rock and roll, skiers hold the grips of the poles close together so their gloves touch. As they plant the poles, they make sure the base of each one is shoulder width apart. They keep their hands waist high and their arms and elbows stiff.

The skiers allow their momentum to straighten the poles perpendicular to the slope. As the poles straighten, the skiers lift themselves from the slope by pushing up with their arms, keeping the pole grips together against their abdomen.

The skiers rock forward slowly so that their skis are between the perpendicular poles. Maintaining their grip, skiers begin the roll by bending at the waist. They bend their knees slightly and bring their heels over their head.

When they are completely upside down, they extend their legs high into the air and continue rolling. They push their body away from their poles and try to touch the ground with their toes. The momentum lands the skis flat on the slope and pulls the poles from the snow.

Rock and roll.

Freestyle Jumping

Of all the freestyle events, nothing can compare to the thrills and excitement of jumping. Jumping is by far the most spectacular event—and the most dangerous.

All potential freestyle jumpers approach these stunts with caution and respect. Safety first is the number one rule. Skiers attending a freestyle camp become familiar with different parts of the jump before actually performing them. The skiers learn the easy jumps first. Then they gradually try more difficult jumps.

Learning to become a successful freestyle jumper takes much practice under lots of supervision. Only when jumping becomes second nature does a skier move on to competition jumping.

Jumping is the most spectacular freestyle event.

Pop and Tuck

The easiest kind of jump is a trail jump. It requires no ramp, just a natural mound of snow. The easiest aerial maneuver is called the pop and tuck.

To perform the pop and tuck, skiers bend their knees as they approach the mound. To launch themselves, skiers pop from the mound by momentarily extending their body. Once airborne, they bring their knees to their chest and tuck the poles under their arm pits. Their thighs rest against their chest and their arms press tightly against their body.

To land, skiers extend their legs just before touchdown. They bend their knees slightly to absorb the shock.

The Spread Eagle

Once skiers become comfortable with the standard pop and tuck jump, they try different maneuvers while airborne. One maneuver is the spread eagle.

Skiers approach the spread eagle jump in the standard manner, with their knees bent. They pop from the jump and keep their upper body and hips facing forward. At the same time, they raise their arms and legs out to the side as if doing a jumping jack.

Performing the spread eagle.

Skiers make sure they spread their arms and legs at the same speed. This helps them retain balance during the jump.

The Twister
The twister is an aerial maneuver where the skiers' upper body faces one way while their lower body faces another.

Once airborne, skiers keep their upper body facing forward. They press their legs tightly together with knees locked. They rotate their skis to one side, then quickly bring them back to the forward position. Throughout the jump, the skis remain flat.

The twister.

The Daffy

When skiers do the splits in the air, they perform the daffy. Skiers keep their upper body facing forward. They extend one leg forward with the ski tip perpendicular to the ground.

At the same time, they extend the other leg back so the ski tip points to the ground. To keep their balance, they extend their arms out to the side.

It is important for skiers to get a strong pop when performing the daffy. If they don't get enough height, their skis might catch the ground. Skiers try to finish the maneuver early in the jump. Otherwise, they may not be able to return their skis to a flat position for a safe landing.

The Backscratcher

When performing the back-scratcher, skiers keep their skis close together while pulling them up behind the back. At all times, skiers keep their upper body facing forward. They bend their knees and bring their heels up behind them so the ski tips point straight down. To maintain good balance, skiers extend their arms out to the side.

The Iron Cross

The iron cross is similar to the backscratcher. The major difference is that the skiers cross the skis behind them instead of parallel to each other.

The Helicopter

The helicopter is one of the most dramatic and complex aerial stunts. The upright skier rotates 360 degrees in the air while the skis remain flat.

Skiers must launch themselves properly from the jump. To rotate in the air, they begin turning just as they leave the lip of the jump. They turn their head, shoulders, and hips while keeping their extended legs close together. The rest of their body follows.

When they have just about completed the 360-degree turn, the skiers open their arms to slow the rotation.

Competition Skiing

After skiers complete extensive training in a freestyle camp, they may consider competition skiing. Before competing, skiers must join the USSA. If you live in Canada, you must join the Canadian Ski Association.

The USSA is recognized by the United States Congress and the Olympic Committee as the only organization that governs all phases of skiing. The Canadian Ski Association governs skiing in Canada. Each association puts together programs and events for freestyle skiers. They also provide licenses that all skiers must obtain before they can compete. There is no age limit for freestyle skiers.

Skiers' first competitions will occur at the state or local level. From there, they can progress to the Regional, National, World Cup, and finally the Olympic Team.

**Snow Skates—The
Latest Craze**

SnowRunner® snow skates are the newest craze to hit the downhill slopes since snowboards. SnowRunner snowskates, which debuted in America in 1991, are thermal-insulated lightweight boots with a built-in ski. They have hard, boot-length plastic skis on the bottoms. Users "skate" down the hill without poles.

Snow skating on SnowRunner snow skates combine techniques used in ice skating, in-line skating, and skiing. This makes it easy to learn and allows users to make sharp turns and do more creative moves than on regular skis. Users can skate, ski, go backwards, and do leg crossovers. And there is no worry about crossing ski tips, which can cause injury.

Snow*Runner* snow skates' average speed is 25 to 30 m.p.h. Skiers can reach speeds in excess of 45 m.p.h. Without a long ski on which to turn, there is no turning or twisting action applied to the lower body—especially the legs.

The idea for Snow*Runner* snow skates dates back to the 1960s. They were the brainchild of Swiss inventor Hannes Jacob. As a child, Jacob would take the heels off his shoes so he could glide over the snowy hills on his way to school. By the late 1970s, it was his dream to make a boot that would allow stable, controlled movement while traveling downhill.

Jacob completed his first design in the early 1980s. But it was heavy and clunky, like downhill ski boots. Jacob continued experimenting and finally came up with a boot that would eventually become the model for the Snow*Runner* snow skate.

In 1986, Jacob received a patent for his invention. Then he sold the rights to Dalbello Sport of Italy. Dalbello is one of the world's largest and oldest ski-boot makers. Two years later, Dalbello developed the first injection moulded boot, and Snow*Runner* snow skates were introduced.

Italian and Swiss skiers were the first to try Snow*Runner* snow skates. Shortly afterward, skiers in Austria, France, and other European countries began to use them.

SnowRunner snow skates are the world's first fully functional snow skiing skates.

SnowRunner snow skates fit looser than regular ski boots. With a ski boot, there are 2 to 3 feet of ski in front and in back of the boot. So, a tight fit is needed. If a skier's foot is not locked in, control is lost. With SnowRunner snow skates, there is not a long ski on which to turn. So a tight-fitting boot is not needed. And there is room for air circulation which keeps the foot warmer.

Boots come in four sizes: extra-small, small, medium, and large. Children can wear the extra-small and small sizes. SnowRunner snow skates cost $250 compared to about $350 to $600 for snowboards with bindings. Skis, poles, and bindings run from $350 to $1,200. SnowRunner snow skates can be found in most major sporting goods stores across the country. Contact SnowRunner (USA) Inc. at **1-800-SKATE ON** for more details.

Ski Associations

For more information about freestyle snow skiing, write to:

The U.S. Ski Association
P.O. Box 100
Park City, Utah 84060

Canadian Ski Association
1600 James Naismith Drive
Gloucester, Ontario, Canada
K1B 5N4

North American Professional
Snowboarders Association
(NAPSA)
2182 Foothill Drive
Vista, California 92084

U.S. Recreational Ski Association
1315 East Pacifico Avenue
Aneheim, California 92805

GLOSSARY

Aerial—in the air.

Amateur—a person who does something just for the pleasure of doing it, not for money.

Choosing a line—visually choosing a course down a ski slope.

Choreography—to arrange or direct the movements of someone.

Freestyle—a competition in which someone uses a style of his or her own choice instead of a specified style.

Mogul—a bump in a ski run.

Mogul shelf—a mogul with a flat top.

Ski run—a slope or trail suitable for skiing.